PRESENTED TO:

_____

FROM:

_____

DATE:

_____

5

ENNEAGRAM TYPE

BETH McCORD

Your **Enneagram** Coach

THOMAS NELSON
Since 1798

Enneagram Type 5: The Investigative Thinker

© 2019 by Beth McCord

Published in Nashville, Tennessee, by Thomas Nelson. Thomas Nelson is a registered trademark of HarperCollins Christian Publishing, Inc.

Published in association with Alive Literary Agency.

Graphic Designer: Jane Butler, Well Refined Creative Director, wellrefined.co
Interior Designer: Emily Ghattas
Cover Designer: Greg Jackson at Thinkpen Design

ISBN-13: 978-1-4002-1573-7

Printed in China

19 20 21 22 23 GRI 10 9 8 7 6 5 4 3 2 1

Contents

Foreword

I'll be honest: my first reaction to being introduced to the whole Enneagram concept was to chortle at it. Have you ever chortled? Fundamentally, it's a very guttural noise, and typically it's done in situations based around authentic and genuine laughter. But in very special circumstances, a chortle can also be weaponized as a divinely obnoxious reaction when you want to dismiss something as patronizingly as possible. And that's what I thought of the Enneagram: something to be looked upon with condescension.

Part of this posture was because I'd been down

the personality-typing road before. And while some of the typing systems contained elementally interesting things to say, as a whole, I found them to be either too vague or too complicated for anything to really take root.

But the other half of my dismissal of the Enneagram was because I didn't think the totality of myself could be captured within a type. I say that at the risk of sounding like a pretentious fart wagon, but it's not something I mean with any kind of pomp or impressive circumstance. It's more about how I recognized how vividly specific I was.

Did I feel like I contained multitudes? Oh yes, you can believe that. I felt like I contained multiple multitudes. But beyond that, I also knew that I was different, and when you designate something as "specific," that's often just a really nice way of saying that it is strange, which is what I felt about myself: strange. And after a while, you get tired of searching for identity in a world that doesn't seem designed to quantify your exact brand of identification. It's better to chortle and dismiss than it is to be constantly reminded of your "specificity."

But then I took an Enneagram test, where I was revealed to be Type 5.

During my investigation about what it means to be Type 5, I was moved to tears (a rare event for most 5s to be sure). The tears came because, for the first time, I felt like I could see my identity reflected back to me on the page. And I was absolutely overjoyed by this.

Not overjoyed because I was self-obsessed but because I finally had some hope for better understanding why I am the way I am. I'd always been able to cobble together a justification for myself but never an explanation. But after reading about what makes a Type 5, an explanation finally seemed attainable.

Which is what I love most about the Enneagram. It revealed not just my "how" but also my "why," and in doing so, it gave me a toolbox of language with which to not only better understand myself but also to better help others understand me. And for 5s, who tend toward solitude and isolation, this was a most wonderful kind of gift that I would never dream of chortling at.

Knox McCoy, Cohost, *The Popcast* and *The Bible Binge*; Author, *The Wondering Years*

Introduction

I'm so glad you're here! As an Enneagram teacher and coach, I have seen so many lives changed by the Enneagram. This is a perfect place for you to start your own journey of growth. I'll explain how this interactive book works, but first I'd like to share a little of my story.

Before I learned about the Enneagram, I often unknowingly committed *assumicide*, which is my word for damaging a relationship by assuming I know someone's thoughts, feelings, and motivations. I incorrectly surmise why someone is behaving a particular way and respond (sometimes with disastrous results) without asking clarifying questions to confirm my assumptions or to find out what actually is going on. I've made many wrong and hurtful assumptions about people I dearly love, as well as destructive presumptions about myself.

When my husband, Jeff, and I were in the early years of our marriage, it was a difficult season in our relationship. For the life of me, I couldn't figure out Jeff, or myself. I had been a Christian since I was young and desired to live like Christ, but I kept running into the same stumbling blocks over and over again. I was constantly frustrated, and I longed to understand my heart's motives—*Why do I do what I do?* I figured understanding that might help jolt me out of my rut, but I didn't know where to start.

Then I learned about the insightful tool of the Enneagram, and it was exactly what I needed.

This personality typology (*ennea* for nine; *gram* for diagram) goes beyond what we do (our behaviors) and gets at *why* we do what we do (our heart's motives). And though there are just nine basic personality Types, each Type has multiple layers, allowing for numerous variations of any given personality Type.

The purpose of the Enneagram is to awaken self-awareness and provide hope for growth. Once we learn why each Type thinks, feels, and acts in specific ways, we can look at ourselves with new understanding. Then we can depend on God in new ways to reshape us. The Enneagram makes us aware of when our heart's motives are good and we are on the best path for our personality Type, and when our heart is struggling and veering off course. The Enneagram is an insightful tool, but God's truth is what sets us free and brings transformation.

When I first learned about the Enneagram, I resonated with the Type 9—and had a good laugh when I discovered that 9s know themselves the least! But I finally had wisdom that cleared away the fog and illuminated my inner world. I kept thinking, *Oh, that's why I do that!* Everything started making sense, which brought my restless heart relief.

The Enneagram also helped me see when my heart was aligned with God's truth, misaligned to some degree, or out of alignment entirely with the person God created me to be. It would highlight where I was misunderstanding myself or those I love, and then I could use that awareness to seek transformation. Using the Enneagram from this perspective was a significant turning point for me in all my relationships, especially my marriage. My new perspective allowed me to have more compassion, kindness, forgiveness, mercy, and grace toward others and myself.

Exploring my heart has been some of the hardest—and most rewarding—work I've ever done. The process of looking at our hearts exposes who we are at the core, which highlights our need for redemption and care from God, who is always supplying us with what we need. We simply need to come to Him and depend on Him to change us from the inside out. He will give us a new internal peace, joy, and security that will help us to flourish in new and life-giving ways. The Enneagram can function as an internal GPS, helping you understand why you and others think, feel, and behave in particular ways.

This internal GPS assists you in knowing your current location (your Main Enneagram Type) and your Type's healthiest destination (how your Type can live in alignment with the gospel).

The Enneagram also acts like a rumble strip on the highway—that boundary that makes an irritating sound when your car touches it, warning you when you're about to go off course. It keeps you from swerving into dangerous situations.

While everyone has character traits of all nine Types to varying degrees, we call only one our Main Type. In this book you will unlock some of the mysteries behind *why* you do what you do and discern ways you can grow into your best self.

If you're not sure of your Type number, that's okay! Going through the exercises will help you figure out what your Type number is. Sometimes it's helpful to find out what we're *not* as much as what we are. It's all about self-discovery and self-awareness.

If you find you resonate more with another number, that insight is valuable.

· · ·

In the twenty-one entries that follow, we'll begin with a summary of your Type. Then we'll discuss topics that are general to the Enneagram and specific to your Type. Each reading will end with reflection questions—prompts to help you write out your thoughts, feelings, and gut reactions to what you have read. Putting pen to paper will help you focus and process what is going on inside you.

Before you begin, I want you to commit to observing your inner world from a nonjudgmental stance. Since God has fully forgiven us, we can observe ourselves without condemnation, guilt, or shame. Instead, we can rest in the fact that we are unconditionally loved, forgiven, and accepted based on what Christ did for us. Follow the prompts and write about your own story. Allow God to transform you from the inside out by helping you see yourself through the lens of the beautiful and amazing Type He designed you to be.

It's my privilege to walk with you as you discover who you are by examining your heart. I'm excited to be on this journey with you!

You are profoundly perceptive and capable of original, brilliant, and inventive solutions to problems. You can comfortably stand back and view life objectively, come to a complete understanding, and make decisions based on reason and knowledge without getting tangled up in your emotions.

OVERVIEW OF THE NINE ENNEAGRAM TYPES

The Enneagram (*ennea* = nine, *gram* = diagram) is a map for personal growth that identifies the nine basic ways of relating to and perceiving the world. It accurately describes *why* you think, feel, and behave in particular ways based upon your Core Motivations. Understanding the Enneagram will give you more self-awareness, forgiveness, and compassion for yourself and others.

To find your main Type, take our FREE assessment at test.YourEnneagramCoach.com, and find the Type on the next page that has your Core Motivations— what activates and drives your thoughts, feelings, and behaviors.

Core Motivations of Each Type

 Core Desires: what you're always striving for, believing it will completely fulfill you

 Core Fears: what you're always avoiding and trying to prevent from happening

 Core Weakness: the issue you're always wrestling with, which will remain a struggle until you're in heaven and is a reminder you need God's help on a daily basis

 Core Longing: the message your heart is always longing to hear

Type 1: MORAL PERFECTIONIST

 Core Desire: Having integrity; being good, balanced, accurate, virtuous, and right.

 Core Fear: Being wrong, bad, evil, inappropriate, unredeemable, or corruptible.

 Core Weakness: *Resentment*: Repressing anger that leads to continual frustration and dissatisfaction with yourself, others, and the world for not being perfect.

 Core Longing: You are good.

Type 2: SUPPORTIVE ADVISOR

☀ **Core Desire:** Being appreciated, loved, and wanted.

▼ **Core Fear:** Being rejected and unwanted; being thought worthless, needy, inconsequential, dispensable, or unworthy of love.

 Core Weakness: *Pride*: Denying your own needs and emotions while using your strong intuition to discover and focus on the emotions and needs of others; confidently inserting your helpful support in hopes that others will say how grateful they are for your thoughtful care.

🔥 **Core Longing:** You are wanted and loved.

Type 3: SUCCESSFUL ACHIEVER

☀ **Core Desire:** Having high status and respect; being admired, successful, and valuable.

▼ **Core Fear:** Being exposed as or thought incompetent, inefficient, or worthless; failing to be or appear successful.

 Core Weakness: *Deceit*: Deceiving yourself into believing that you are only the image you present to others; embellishing the truth by putting on a polished persona for everyone (including yourself) to see and admire.

🔥 **Core Longing:** You are loved for simply being you.

Type 4: ROMANTIC INDIVIDUALIST

☀ **Core Desire:** Being unique, special, and authentic.

▼ **Core Fear:** Being inadequate, emotionally cut off, plain, mundane, defective, flawed, or insignificant.

⌘ **Core Weakness:** *Envy:* Feeling that you're tragically flawed, that something foundational is missing inside you, and that others possess qualities you lack.

🔥 **Core Longing:** You are seen and loved for exactly who you are—special and unique.

Type 5: INVESTIGATIVE THINKER

☀ **Core Desire:** Being capable and competent.

▼ **Core Fear:** Being annihilated, invaded, or not existing; being thought incapable or ignorant; having obligations placed upon you, or your energy being completely depleted.

⌘ **Core Weakness:** *Avarice:* Feeling that you lack inner resources and that too much interaction with others will lead to catastrophic depletion; withholding yourself from contact with the world; holding on to your resources and minimizing your needs.

🔥 **Core Longing:** Your needs are not a problem.

Type 6: LOYAL GUARDIAN

 Core Desire: Having security, guidance, and support.

Core Fear: Fearing fear itself; being without support, security, or guidance; being blamed, targeted, alone, or physically abandoned.

Core Weakness: *Anxiety*: Scanning the horizon of life and trying to predict and prevent negative outcomes (especially worst-case scenarios); remaining in a constant state of apprehension and worry.

Core Longing: You are safe and secure.

Type 7: ENTERTAINING OPTIMIST

Core Desire: Being happy, fully satisfied, and content.

Core Fear: Being deprived, trapped in emotional pain, limited, or bored; missing out on something fun.

Core Weakness: *Gluttony*: Feeling a great emptiness inside and having an insatiable desire to "fill yourself up" with experiences and stimulation in hopes of feeling completely satisfied and content.

Core Longing: You will be taken care of.

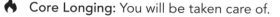

Type 8: PROTECTIVE CHALLENGER

☀ **Core Desire:** Protecting yourself and those in your inner circle.

⚠ **Core Fear:** Being weak, powerless, harmed, controlled, vulnerable, manipulated, and left at the mercy of injustice.

⁉ **Core Weakness:** *Lust/Excess*: Constantly desiring intensity, control, and power; willfully pushing yourself on others in order to get what you desire.

🔥 **Core Longing:** You will not be betrayed.

Type 9: PEACEFUL MEDIATOR

☀ **Core Desire:** Having inner stability and peace of mind.

⚠ **Core Fear:** Being in conflict, tension, or discord; feeling shut out and overlooked; losing connection and relationship with others.

⁉ **Core Weakness:** *Sloth*: Remaining in an unrealistic and idealistic world in order to keep the peace, remain easygoing, and not be disturbed by your anger; falling asleep to your passions, abilities, desires, needs, and worth by merging with others to keep peace and harmony.

🔥 **Core Longing:** Your presence matters.

TYPE 5

KEY MOTIVATIONS

Type 5s are motivated to be capable and competent, to master skills and areas of knowledge, to explore, to remain undisturbed by others, and to reduce their reliance on others.

Overview of Type 5

The Investigative Thinker

Perceptive | Insightful | Intelligent
Detached | Isolated

You are a perceptive observer who walks through life with curiosity and a craving to learn new things. You are innovative, objective, and practical, making wise decisions based on reason and knowledge.

Despite your insatiable thirst for thinking and knowing, you experience the world as an intrusive and overwhelming place. Feeling that life demands too much of you, you focus your attention on conserving your energy to avoid a sense of catastrophic depletion. This intense desire to hoard your internal resources and control your environment can damage your relationships as you can become extremely private and emotionally distant.

When you attempt to navigate life apart from God, your fear of not knowing or being enough, combined with your desire for self-sufficiency, can cause you to withdraw from others and be emotionally distant. You fear feeling incompetent and often think you must know everything before sharing your insights, which overwhelms you and causes you to retreat.

This desire for knowledge, independence, and a life free from obligations can strain your relationships since connection, feelings, and vulnerability are components of healthy partnerships. You distance yourself from the demands of living in relationship with others because you feel ill-equipped to meet them. You think confidence to engage with others will come, but you never feel you have enough knowledge or resources to enter into the mysterious and complex world of another person.

However, when your heart aligns with God's truth, you discover that your needs are not a problem because God can meet them. Then you can begin to be more generous with giving of yourself and your resources to others, moving from a fear of scarcity to a belief in abundance. You start living not just from your head but also from your heart and the whole of who you are. That, combined with your great vision and perspective, offers true wisdom to the world.

Faith and the Enneagram

Is your heart a mystery to you? Do you need help using the knowledge the Enneagram offers to improve your life? If that's where you are, I'm happy to tell you that there is help and there is hope.

The Bible teaches that God cares about our heart's motives. He "sees not as man sees: man looks on the outward appearance, but the Lᴏʀᴅ looks on the heart" (1 Samuel 16:7). So we shouldn't look only at our external behaviors; we also need to examine our inner world. For most of us, it's no surprise that the heart of our problem is the problem of our heart!

Before we begin discussing the Enneagram in depth, I'd like to share my beliefs with you for two reasons: First, it's a critical part of how I'll guide you through the Enneagram principles. Second, my faith is what sustains and encourages me, and I believe the same will be true for you.

I believe the Bible is God's truth and the ultimate authority for our lives. Through it, we learn about God's character, love, and wisdom. It brings us close to Him and guides us in the best way to live. My relationship with God brought me healing and purpose before I ever heard of the Enneagram.

Jesus has not been optional for my personal growth; He has been absolutely and utterly vital. He has always come alongside me with love, compassion, and mercy.

I've always wanted my faith to be the most important part of my life, but I spent years frustrated, running into the same issues in my heart over and over again. The Enneagram helped me understand my heart's motives.

As you think about your Type, I'll help you look at

your heart, your life, and your relationships through the lens of the Enneagram. I'll also teach you ways to understand yourself and others and to develop patience and empathy for your differences.

With God working in you and helpful insights from the Enneagram to change awareness and actions, you'll grow into the person you'd like to be more than you've ever dared to dream possible.

When you place your faith in Jesus Christ as your Savior, three life-changing questions are answered, bringing you ultimate grace and freedom:

Am I fully accepted by God (even with all the mess and sin in my life)?

Yes! You are declared righteous. Christ not only purchased forgiveness for your sin but also gave you His perfect righteousness.

Am I loved by God?

Yes! God cherishes you and wants you to be close to Him. He adopted you, making you His beloved child.

Is it really possible for me to change?

Yes! You are being made new. This both *happened* to you and *is happening* to you. This means that you are changed because of what Christ has done, and you are continuing to change as you grow in Christ (it's a bit of a paradox). You can live in an ongoing process of growth by working with the Holy Spirit to become more like Christ, who loves you and gave Himself up for you.

These three life-changing events are what we mean by God's truth, the good news of Christ's finished work on our behalf—"the gospel."

Receiving God's truth and learning about the Enneagram will give you a deeper and richer understanding of *who you are* and *Whose you are*.

When we know *who we are*, we understand our heart's motives and needs and can see God reaching out to meet our needs and giving us grace for our sins through Christ.

And when we know *Whose we are*, we understand that, because of Christ's sacrifice on our behalf, we're God's cherished children. He comforts, sustains, and delights in us. Because of God's character, His love never changes; it doesn't depend on us "getting better" or "doing better" since it hinges solely on what Christ has already done for us. He loves us and desires for us to be in a relationship with Him. We become more like Him by surrendering to Him and depending on the Holy Spirit to transform us.

Which leads us back to looking at who we are. Bringing our faith and the Enneagram together helps us hear God's truths in our mother tongue (kind of like our personality Type's unique language), which enables us to understand God's truth more deeply and will lead to transformation.

Going Deeper

What things have you longed to change about yourself?

_____

_____

_____

_____

_____

_____

_____

How have you attempted to rescue yourself in the past or bring about change on your own? How successful were you?

_____

_____

_____

_____

What difference does knowing you belong to God make in your life?

Being Aware

We can't do anything to make God love us more or love us less since our relationship status has been taken care of solely through Christ's finished work on our behalf. And yet that doesn't mean we're not responsible for participating in our growth. That growth path will look different for different personality Types. We can use the Enneagram to help us find our unique path for transformation as we continue learning and growing. And that's what's super fun about the Enneagram! This insightful tool helps us discover *who we are* and *Whose we are.*

We are not alone on this journey of growth.

God is with us, sustaining us and providing for us. Although we're all uniquely made and no one is alike (it boggles the mind to think about it!), there are commonalities in how we think, feel, and act. The Enneagram shows us nine basic personality Types, each with its own specific patterns of thinking and ways of being: nine *valid* perspectives of the world. Getting to know each of these personality Types increases understanding, compassion, mercy, grace, and forgiveness toward ourselves and others.

Our creative God made us so diverse, yet we all reflect the essence of His character: wise, caring, radiant, creative, knowledgeable, insightful, joyful, protective, and peaceful. As we learn about ourselves and others from the Enneagram, we also learn more about God. Our strengths reflect His attributes.

So how do we begin to find our unique path for growth? By learning about the Enneagram, and by becoming aware of how our heart is doing, which isn't always easy for us. It takes a great deal of time and intentional focus. We start by observing our inner world from a *nonjudgmental* stance. (I don't know how to emphasize this enough!)

Then we can begin to recognize patterns, pause while we are in the present circumstance, and ask ourselves good, clarifying questions about *why* we are thinking, feeling, or behaving in particular ways. We can begin to identify those frustrating patterns we repeat over and over again (the ones we haven't been able to figure out how to stop) and start to think about why we keep doing them.

As I've said before, the Enneagram can act like a rumble strip on a highway, warning you when you're heading off your best path. It lets you know that if you continue in the same direction, drowsy or distracted, you might hurt yourself and others. Alerts about impending danger allow you to course correct, avoid heartache, and experience greater freedom. You will create new patterns of behavior, including a new way of turning to God, when you start to notice the rumble strips in your life.

When you're sensing a rumble strip warning, focus on the acronym AWARE:

- *Awaken*: Notice how you are reacting in your behavior, feelings, thoughts, and body sensations.
- *Welcome*: Be open to what you might learn and observe without condemnation and shame.
- *Ask*: Ask God to help clarify what is happening internally.
- *Receive*: Receive any insight and affirm your true identity as God's beloved child.
- *Enjoy*: Enjoy your new freedom from old self-defeating patterns of living.

Going Deeper

As you look back on your life, when would you have liked a rumble strip to warn you of danger?

_____

_____

_____

_____

_____

_____

In general, what causes you to veer off course and land in a common pitfall (for example, when you're worried)?

_____

_____

_____

_____

_____

SHARING WITH OTHERS
HOW BEST TO LOVE ME

Do not be clingy or overly emotional
but instead be independent,
rational, and resourceful.

Please speak in a short, straightforward,
and concise manner.

Interactions with people drain my
inner resources to the point that I feel
as though I will suffer catastrophic
depletion. Therefore, I need a lot of
alone time to recharge and process
my feelings and thoughts.

I don't like surprises, intrusions, or
clingy, needy, and overly emotional
people. These quickly deplete me.

Core Motivations

We'll begin discussing the fundamentals of the Enneagram by looking at our motivations.

Your Core Motivations are the driving force behind your thoughts, feelings, and actions. The internal motivations specific to your Type help explain why you do what you do. (This is why it's impossible to discern someone else's Type. We don't know what motivates them to think, feel, and behave in particular ways. It's their Core Motivations, not their actions, that determine their Type.)

These Core Motivations consist of:

- *Core Fear*: what you're always avoiding and trying to prevent from happening
- *Core Desire*: what you're always striving for, believing it will completely fulfill you
- *Core Weakness*: the issue you're always wrestling with, which will remain a struggle until you're in heaven and is a reminder you need God's help on a daily basis
- *Core Longing*: the message your heart longs to hear

The Enneagram, like a nonjudgmental friend, names and addresses these dynamics of your heart. When you use the Enneagram from a faith-centered approach, you can see how Christ's finished work on your behalf has already satisfied your Core Longing and resolved your Core Fear, Core Desire, and Core Weakness. It's a process to learn how to live in that reality.

When we stray from the truth that we are God's beloved children, it's harder to look inside. After all,

Scripture tells us that "the heart is deceitful . . . and desperately sick" (Jeremiah 17:9). When we forget God's unconditional love for us, we respond to our weaknesses and vulnerabilities with shame or contempt, leaving us feeling worse.

When we only focus on obeying externally, we attempt to look good on the outside but never deal with the source of all our struggles on the inside.

However, when we allow ourselves to rest in the truth that Christ took care of everything for us, we can look at our inner world without fear or condemnation. Real transformation begins when we own our shortcomings.

Here are the Core Motivations of a Type 5:

- *Core Fear*: being annihilated, invaded, or not existing; being thought incapable or ignorant; having obligations placed upon you, or your energy being completely depleted
- *Core Desire*: being capable and competent

- *Core Weakness*: avarice; feeling that you lack inner resources and that too much interaction with others will lead to catastrophic depletion; withholding yourself from contact with the world; holding on to your resources and minimizing your needs
- *Core Longing*: "Your needs are not a problem."

The Enneagram exposes the condition of our hearts, and it will tear down any facade we try to hide behind. Since we are God's saved children, we don't have to be afraid of judgment. We can be vulnerable because we know God has taken care of us perfectly through Christ—He has forgiven us and set us free from fear, condemnation, and shame. His presence is a safe place where we can be completely honest about where we are. With this freedom, allow the Enneagram to be a flashlight to your heart's condition. Let it reveal how you are doing at any given moment so you can remain on the best path for your personality Type.

Going Deeper

How challenging is it for you to look at the condition of your heart?

_____

_____

_____

_____

_____

_____

What response do you typically have when you recognize your struggles?

_____

_____

_____

_____

_____

_____

How would you like to respond when the struggles inside you are exposed?

Core Fear

Understanding your Core Fear is the first step in identifying your motivations. Your personality believes it's vital to your well-being that you constantly spend time and energy avoiding this thing you fear. It is the lens through which you see the world, the "reality" you believe. You assume others do, or should, see the world through this lens, and you may become confused and dismayed when they don't.

Your Core Fear as a Type 5 is being annihilated, invaded, or not existing; being thought incapable or ignorant; having obligations placed upon you, or your energy completely depleted.

You don't want to have social or emotional obligations placed on you. You don't want to be surprised, have your secrets shared, or be forced to interact with others beyond what your limited energy reserves will allow.

Even though you fear ignorance and obligations that deplete your energy, here's what is true: God provides you with a never-ending resource of knowledge, understanding, and energy in the Holy Spirit.

God does not withhold good things from His children. He gives willingly and with great delight. He will give you exactly what you need when you need it.

Ask Him for good things, and He will bless you beyond what you can imagine. He wants you to have wisdom, but more than that to trust Him and His provision for you. He gives willingly and with great delight. He does not withhold good things from His children. He will give you the endurance you need when you feel too depleted to keep going. He wants you to trust Him and His provision for you.

When your Core Fears get activated, use them

MY CORE FEARS

TYPE 5
INVESTIGATIVE
THINKER

Being annihilated, invaded, or not existing;
being thought incapable or ignorant;
having obligations placed upon you, or
your energy completely depleted

as a rumble strip to alert you. Then pause, become AWARE, and reorient yourself with what is true so your heart can rest in His provision.

Going Deeper

What comes to mind when you think about your Core Fear?

_____

_____

_____

_____

_____

Do any particular words in the Type 5 Core Fear description ring true for you?

_____

_____

_____

_____

_____

_____

What strategies have you used in the past to
protect yourself from your fears?

_____

_____

_____

_____

_____

_____

_____

_____

_____

_____

_____

_____

_____

Core Desire

Understanding your Core Desire is the next step in identifying your motivations. Your Core Desire is what you're always striving for, believing it will ultimately fulfill you.

While your personality Type is running away from your Core Fear, it's also running toward your Core Desire. You believe that once you have this Core Desire met, all of life will be okay and you will feel fully satisfied and content. This longing to experience your Core Desire constantly propels you to focus your efforts on pursuing and obtaining it.

As a Type 5, you desire to be capable and

competent, to master skills and areas of knowledge, to explore, to remain undisturbed by others, and to reduce your reliance on others.

God knows your Core Desire, and He freely gives it to you. You are not left empty. God restores and refreshes you with His power and wisdom. When you feel you do not have enough information, boldly ask Him to give you faith to move out and try to gain it.

You already have much more knowledge than you realize, so trust in how God designed you and believe He will enable you to recall what you need to when you need to. Also trust that if you don't know something, that it is in God's providence. He will bestow insights to you at the right times so you can trust Him in new ways.

Not everyone has the same Core Desire as you. Take time to recognize that others are just as passionate in obtaining their Core Desire as you are in gaining yours. This awareness will help you navigate relationship dynamics, enabling you to offer more empathy, compassion, and grace. Use

TYPE 5
INVESTIGATIVE
THINKER

Being capable and competent

the Enneagram to know yourself better so you can better communicate with others about what is happening inside your heart. Then be curious about others, and ask them to reveal to you their desires so you can get to know them on a deeper level.

Going Deeper

As you look back over your life, what aspects of the Type 5 Core Desire have you been chasing?

_____

_____

_____

_____

_____

_____

_____

Describe ways you have attempted to pursue these specific desires.

_____

_____

_____

_____

_____

_____

_____

What would it feel like to trust in the fact that God has already completely met your Core Desire?

_____

_____

_____

_____

_____

_____

_____

_____

Core Weakness

Deep inside, you struggle with a Core Weakness, which is your Achilles' heel. This one issue repeatedly causes you to stumble in life. At times you might find some relief. But as hard as you try to improve on your own, your struggle in this area continually resurfaces.

God's encouraging words to you are that when you are weak, He is strong. This brings hope that you are not destined to be utterly stuck in your weakness. As you grow closer to God and depend on Him, He will lessen the constraint your Core Weakness has over you and help you move out of your rut.

As a Type 5, your Core Weakness is *avarice*. You feel that you lack inner resources and that too much interaction with others will lead to catastrophic depletion. So you withhold yourself from contact with the world, holding on to your resources and minimizing your needs.

A Type 5's energy reserves can be compared to the battery life of a cell phone. Extroverts have all the energy they need to interact with people all day long. Introverts can last about 70 to 75 percent of the day, and then they need to go away to plug in and recharge. Type 5s wake up each day with only 20 to 25 percent energy available to interact with people before they experience what feels like catastrophic depletion. Most 5s have a private place where no one is allowed, where they can plug in and recharge.

Others can misinterpret your strong boundaries for privacy as not wanting to be with people, not understanding it is a need to recharge.

God provides you with a spring of living water, constantly flowing with replenishing and renewing strength and wisdom. He delights in delivering what you need. It does not drain Him. Ask Him to care for you and give you real and powerful energy.

By shifting your focus to what God provides for you, you can be more willing to interact with others when you feel low on energy. You can boldly try something, even when you are not sure if you have enough information. He gives you all you need to be confident and assertive.

When you see your Core Weakness surfacing, think of it as a rumble strip, alerting you that you can easily veer off course into your common pitfalls of emotionally detaching, physically isolating yourself, and becoming more secretive and distant. Use this awareness to "recalculate" your inner world so you can get back to your healthiest path.

Going Deeper

What comes to mind as you think about yo⋯ ⋯e ⋯Weakness?

In what ways have you wrestled with emotionally detaching, physically isolating yourself, and becoming more secretive and distant?

What specific things are you facing now that your Core Weakness impacts?

MY CORE WEAKNESS

TYPE 5
INVESTIGATIVE
THINKER

Avarice — feeling that you lack inner resources and that too much interaction with others will lead to catastrophic depletion; withholding yourself from contact with the world; holding on to your resources and minimizing your needs

Core Longing

Your Core Longing is the message your heart is always yearning to receive, what you've craved since you were a child. Throughout life, you've been striving to hear this message from your family members, friends, teachers, coaches, and bosses. No matter how much you've tried to get others to communicate this message to you, you've never felt it was delivered to the degree your heart needed it.

As a Type 5, your Core Longing is to hear, "Your needs are not a problem."

You have believed that if you could be knowledgeable, capable, and competent enough, then others would communicate this message to you, whether in verbal or nonverbal ways. However, even those who have tried their best to do this for you are unable to satisfy this longing that runs so deep inside you.

Why? Because people *cannot* give you all you need. Only God can. When you're trying to receive this message apart from God, you will always thirst for more. But when you listen to Him and see that He's drawing you to Himself, then you will find fulfillment and freedom.

How does God meet your Core Longing?

1. **He sees and takes care of your needs.**

   You do not need to worry that your resources will run out. God knows exactly what you need and provides for you because of His immense love for you.

2. **He restores your empty internal reservoir.**

   God knows that your relational battery gets drained quickly, and you need solitude to recharge. When you seek Him in solitude,

He will fill you and satisfy you. His life-giving power will recharge your energy.

When you feel incompetent and incapable, use the Enneagram as the rumble strip to alert you of what is true: that God can restore you. Allow it to point out how you are believing false messages so you can live a more abundant and connected life.

Going Deeper

How have you seen your Core Longing at work in your life?

_____

_____

_____

_____

_____

_____

What did that look like when you were a child?

_____

_____

_____

_____

_____

_____

_____

_____

_____

_____

How does it appear in your life as an adult?

_____

_____

_____

_____

_____

_____

Describe how you feel and what you think when you read that God answers your longing.

MY CORE LONGING

TYPE 5
INVESTIGATIVE
THINKER

The message my heart always longs to hear.

"Your needs are not
a problem."

Directional Signals of the Enneagram

Just as a GPS gives directional signals such as "Approaching right turn" or "Proceed to the high-lighted route," the Enneagram guides us in which way to go. But we still need to pay attention to where we're heading and reroute our course when necessary.

The Enneagram provides directions in a couple of ways: (1) by pointing out how aligned with God's truth we are, and (2) by showing us what other Types we are connected to and how we might take on those Types' characteristics in different life situations. We do not *become* the Types we are

YOUR INTERNAL GPS

It reveals **why** you think, feel, and behave in particular ways, so you can steer your internal life in the best direction for your personality Type.

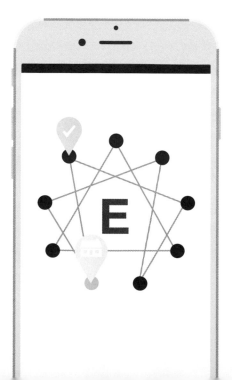

connected to; we remain our Main Type (with its Core Fear, Desire, Weakness, and Longing) as we access the other Types' attributes.

The directional signals of the Enneagram make us aware of which way our heart is heading and where we might end up. Whether it's a good or bad direction depends on various factors—it can change day by day as we take on positive or negative qualities of other Types.

When we are headed in the wrong direction, the steps to turning around and getting back on track are simply owning our mistakes, turning from them, asking for forgiveness from God and others, and asking God to restore us to the best path.

The directional signals we'll discuss in the following entries are: the Levels of Alignment with God's Truth, the Wings, the Triads, and the Enneagram Paths. Hang in there! I'll guide you through these signals, which will help you discover who you are and Whose you are, and show you the healthiest path for your personality Type.

Type 5   HOW I TYPICALLY COMMUNICATE

When I am doing well, I am respectful, nonintrusive, curious, observant, and I engage in stimulating conversations with others.

When I am not doing well, I can be overly brief, cold, and intellectually arrogant. I might withdraw or detach when I feel relational obligations placed on me.

Levels of Alignment with God's Truth

The first set of directional signals we'll discuss are the Levels of Alignment with God's truth. The inspiration for these levels comes from the apostle Paul, who wrote in Galatians 2:14 that some of the early Christian leaders' conduct was not in step (aligned) with God's truth. To grow in our particular personality Type, we must be in step with God's truth and design for us.

We all move fluidly through the Levels of Alignment from day to day. The level at which we find ourselves at any given moment depends on our heart's condition and how we're navigating through life.

Healthy	Aligned with God's Truth (Living as His Beloved)
Average (Autopilot)	Misaligned with God's Truth (Living in Our Own Strength)
Unhealthy	Out of Alignment with God's Truth (Living as an Orphan)

When we are resting, believing, and trusting in who we are in Christ, we are living as His beloved (healthy and aligned with God's truth). We are no longer using our personality strategies to meet our needs and desires. Instead, we are coming to our God, who we know loves us and will provide for us.

When our heart and mind begin to wander from that truth, we start to believe that we must take some control and live in our own strength, even though He is good and sovereign (average/auto-pilot level).

Then there are times when we completely forget that we are His beloved children. In this state of mind, we think we're all alone, that we're orphans who have to handle all of life on our own (unhealthy level).

But no matter where we are on the Levels of Alignment, we are always His cherished children. Christ's life, death, and resurrection accomplished everything required for us to be His. Therefore, no matter what state our heart is in, we can *rejoice* in His work in our lives, *repent* if we need to, and fully *rest* in who we are in Him.

As you can imagine, a group of people with the same personality Type (same Core Fear, Desire, Weakness, and Longing) can look vastly different from each other due to varying alignments with God's truth.

In the readings that follow, we will consider how you as a Type 5 function at the three Levels of Alignment.

Going Deeper

At what Level of Alignment do you think your heart is at the moment?

_____

_____

_____

_____

_____

_____

_____

_____

_____

In what season of life have you thrived the most, not feeling limited by your fears and weaknesses?

_____

_____

_____

What do you think contributed to that growth?

When You Are Aligned

When the condition of your heart is healthy, you align with God's truth that you are fully taken care of by Christ.

As a Type 5 at this level, you observe all parts of life with incredible insight and wisdom. You see things that most people do not notice. When you use these gifts with expertise, you can bring about great innovation and radical change that benefits the world.

You feel deeply connected with yourself and others. Because of this connection, you often use your knowledge and insights to help others. You bless people by contributing through researching, learning, and pioneering new technologies, fields of study, or inventions that bring about good.

Relationally, you can remain present longer without needing to withdraw as frequently. Becoming less guarded and more attached to your emotions, you embrace a new kind of wisdom apart from your mind, utilizing your other capacities and senses. This allows you to experience and understand life more fully, bringing about even greater wisdom and knowledge.

Going Deeper

When are you at your best and most trusting of God?

What differences do you notice in your thinking
and in your life when you're in that state?

What helps you stay in alignment with God's plan
for your personality Type?

Write about a time when you've remained present longer without needing to withdraw as frequently, or any other indicators of healthy alignment.

When You Are Misaligned

Even though we know God is good and in control, there are times when our hearts and minds wander away from the truth that God loves us and has fully provided for us in the finished work of Christ on our behalf. In this average or autopilot level of health, we start to believe that we must take some control and live in our own strength.

As a Type 5 at this level, you believe you cannot share your needs with others for fear of being rejected or overwhelmed by interpersonal connection.

Developing strong boundaries to protect yourself from people becoming too invasive, you withdraw and remain private, guarded, and autonomous. You may

MY HIDDEN STRUGGLE
TYPE 5

The fear of going deep with others and coming to rely on their affection, putting my independence at risk

The belief that my needs would be too intense or harmful if openly expressed to others

The feeling that the competency and self-reliance I work so hard to maintain will be compromised if I enter into deep relationships

obsess overworking things out in your mind, conceptualizing and fine-tuning. You also detach from your emotions and hoard your internal resources to avoid being depleted.

As you become increasingly detached from others, you may be overly involved with complicated ideas or imaginary worlds in your mind. You may take a cynical, argumentative, or antagonistic stance toward anything that would interfere with your inner world and personal visions.

Going Deeper

What aspects of your behavior and life indicate that you are becoming misaligned?

In what ways do you attempt to live in your own strength, not in your identity as a person God loves?

What can you do when you begin to catch yourself in misalignment?

When You Are Out of Alignment Entirely

When we completely forget that our status never changes and we are still His beloved based on what Christ did for us, we think and believe we're all alone, like an orphan.

Your whole world at this level revolves around withdrawing, isolating from others, and hoarding your resources, forgetting that God will provide new resources when you give yours away to others. Your mind lingers on your imaginings, and you become frightened by your deep, haunting, and conspiratorial thinking.

You may become reclusive and isolated from

reality, rejecting and pushing others away and disengaging from all social attachments. You fear that others are planning to harm you. So, before others can harm you, you begin to plan ways to harm them. Your thoughts can become so skewed that you experience distortions of truth and even hallucinations. You may become severely depressed and detached from reality. Life itself seems too intrusive and depleting.

This cycle will continue until you realize the depth of God's love for you and His desire to meet your needs. When you grasp this truth, you will move up the levels of health.

Going Deeper

In what seasons of life have you been most out of alignment with God's truth?

_____

_____

_____

_____

_____

_____

What does this level look like for you (specific behaviors, beliefs, etc.)?

_____

_____

_____

_____

_____

_____

Who in your life can best support and encourage you when you're struggling and guide you back to health?

The Wings

The next set of directional signals we'll discuss are the Wings, which are the two numbers *directly* next to your Main Type's number on the Enneagram diagram. As I've said, we access the characteristics of the Type on either side of us while remaining our Main Type. So everyone's Enneagram personality is a combination of one Main Type and the two Types adjacent to it.

As a Type 5, your Wings are 4 and 6. You'll often see it written this way: 5w4 or 5w6.

Everyone uses their Wings to varying degrees and differently in different circumstances, but it's common for a person to rely more on one Wing than another.

You can think of the Wings like salt and pepper. Each Wing adds a unique "flavor" to your personality, bringing complexity to your Main Type. Just as a delicious filet mignon doesn't *become* the salt or pepper we season it with, we don't become our Wings. Our Wings influence our Main Type in varying ways, both positively and negatively depending on where we are on the Levels of Alignment. We know that too much salt or pepper can make that filet inedible, but the right balance can enhance our enjoyment of it significantly.

When we align with God's truth, we can access the healthy aspects of our Wings. When we are misaligned or out of alignment with God's truth, we will often draw from the average or unhealthy aspects of our Wings. And like under seasoning or over seasoning our perfectly cooked steaks, it can make a huge difference.

Learning how to use our Wings correctly can dramatically alter our life experiences. Applying "seasoning"—utilizing the healthy attributes of our Wings—can help us change course. As we return to believing and trusting in God, we can express ourselves more fully and be seen for who we really are.

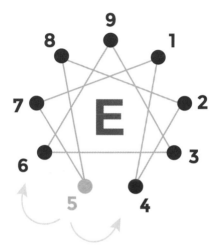

Type 5 with Wing 4 (5w4), The Iconoclast: Both of these Types are withdrawn, so this subtype moves inward to the intellect and emotions. Type 5 lacks the confidence to do, and Type 4 feels something is fundamentally missing internally. This makes it difficult for them to connect with people, and they need time alone to recharge.

If you're an Iconoclast, you can be sociable and desire to know the deep inner world of others from a cerebral stance. You are great at pulling things apart and then conceptualizing new ways to look at them, offering a creative viewpoint. You use your imagination and emotions more than the Problem Solver and can be mistyped as a Type 4.

When you are struggling, you may detach from others by using your intellectual insights and observations to create distance (but you are more sensitive than others realize).

Type 5 with Wing 6 (5w6), The Problem-Solver: This is the subtype we associate Type 5 with most often: intellectual and cerebral. Type 5 desires mastery in a field, and Type 6 desires clarity, which results in incredible research and problem-solving skills.

If you're a Problem-Solver, you thrive in dissecting problems, analyzing them, and finding a solution through your research and intellectual power.

When you are struggling, intimate and personal relationships can be difficult since you mainly live

 **WINGS**

Type 5 with 4 Wing (5w4)
"The Iconoclast"
They tend to be more creative, humanistic, sensitive, empathetic, withdrawn, and self-absorbed.

Type 5 with 6 Wing (5w6)
"The Problem Solver"
They are more extroverted, loyal, anxious, skeptical, cautious, and tend to be interested in the sciences.

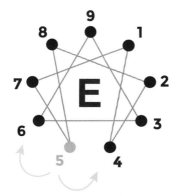

in your mind and not your emotions. Type 6 brings angst and anxiety, which causes Type 5 to detach from others.

Going Deeper

Which Wing do you use more?

_____

_____

_____

_____

_____

_____

How have you seen this Wing enhance your Main Type?

_____

_____

How does it impact your relationships, work, and everyday life?

How does the other Wing influence your Main Type?

_____

_____

_____

_____

_____

_____

_____

_____

How can you utilize it more to create balance?

_____

_____

_____

_____

_____

_____

_____

_____

_____

The Triads

The next set of directional signals we'll discuss are the Triads. We can group the nine personality Types in many ways, and the most common one is by group-ings of three, or Triads. The three Types in each group share common assets and liabilities. For each person one Triad is more dominant (the one with your Main Type) than the other two.

Though we could name several different Triads within the Enneagram, the best known is the Center of Intelligence Triad:

- Feeling Center (Heart Triad): Types 2, 3, and 4
- Thinking Center (Head Triad): Types 5, 6, and 7
- Instinctive Center (Gut Triad): Types 8, 9, and 1

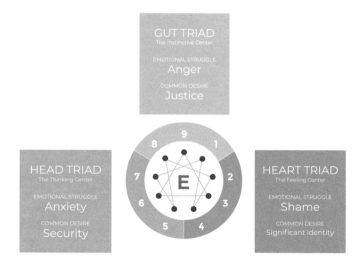

Two commonalities drive the Enneagram Types in each of these three centers: a common emotional imbalance and a common desire.

In the Head Triad, Types 5, 6, and 7 are imbalanced in their *thinking*. They all have similar assets and liabilities related to how they think and engage in life through mental analysis. They all react to their *mental struggles* with *anxiety* (or fear). Type 5s are anxious about not knowing enough to go out into the world and do. Type 6s are anxious about all the negative possibilities that could happen in any given situation. Type 7s are anxious about being forced to focus on their inner world, getting trapped in emotional pain, or feeling deprived.

Those in the Head Triad focus on a desire for *security*. Type 5s seek security through knowledge and understanding. Type 6s seek security in identifying all possible scenarios, planning for all contingencies, and having a support system in place. Type 7s seek security by avoiding their internal world of anxiety and experiencing fun, stimulation, and excitement from the external world.

When you are healthy as a Type 5, you are profoundly perceptive and capable of original, brilliant, and inventive solutions to problems.

However, when you are struggling, you feel more secure in your imaginings and thoughts instead of applying your knowledge. Your life can begin to unravel when you get lost in your mind.

Fearful that you are unable to do things well, you spend a great deal of time thinking, studying, and preparing, though you often don't feel you have enough information to assert yourself confidently and move forward. You constantly feel the need to learn more.

ENNEAGRAM TYPE 5

At Their Best	At Their Worst
Analytical	Intellectually Arrogant
Persevering	Stingy
Sensitive	Stubborn
Wise	Distant
Objective	Critical of Others
Perceptive	Unassertive
Curious	Cynical
Observant	Isolated
Insightful	Relationally Distant

To you, the world is overwhelming and threatening, so you retreat to feel more secure. You then observe the world from a detached, cerebral, and outsider view.

Going Deeper

What stands out to you about being in the Thinking Triad and your propensity for mental analysis?

How attuned are you to your feelings and gut instincts in comparison to thinking?

In what ways do you wrestle with anxiety and constantly feel the need to learn more?

How do you respond to these struggles? Do your actions bring the security you want?

Where do your strengths of observing, learning, and mentally categorizing information shine the most?

Childhood Message

Before we discuss the last set of directional signals (the Enneagram Paths), we need to understand what the Enneagram calls a Childhood Message.

From birth, everyone has a unique perspective on life, our personality Type's perspective. We all tend toward particular assumptions or concerns, and these develop into a Childhood Message. Our parents, teachers, and authority figures may have directly communicated this message to us, but most of the time, we interpreted what they said or did through the lens of our personality Type to fit this belief.

Sometimes we can see a direct correlation

between our Childhood Message and a childhood event; other times we can't. Somewhere, somehow, we picked up a message that rang true for us because of our personality Type's hardwiring. This false interpretation of our circumstances was and still is painful to us, profoundly impacting us as children and as adults.

Gaining insight into how our personality Type interpreted events and relationships in childhood will help us identify how that interpretation is impacting us today. Believing our Childhood Message causes our personality to reinforce its strategies to protect us from our Core Fear—apart from God's truth. Once we understand that the message is hardwired into our thinking, we can experience God's healing truth and live more freely.

What's more, when we know the Childhood Message of others, we can begin to understand why they do what they do and how we can communicate with them more effectively.

As a Type 5, your Childhood Message is: "It is not okay to be too comfortable."

The message your heart longed to hear as a child is your Core Longing: "Your needs aren't a problem."

· · ·

Type 5 children tended to feel rejected, so social interactions and relationships were difficult for them. They often felt awkward and misunderstood by people and preferred to stand back and observe rather than get actively involved. They could seem aloof or caught up in their thoughts. To feel competent and capable, Type 5s gravitated toward specializing in an area of knowledge that interested them.

Viewing the world as intrusive and overwhelming and their parents as overbearing, they withdrew into their private world to escape feeling intruded upon. They did this by retreating into their minds to sort through their thoughts and feelings. They strongly preferred being alone, enjoying the freedom to engage in their interests.

Type 5 children would feel embarrassed if they did not know something about a topic and overwhelmed when others paid too much attention to them or invaded their privacy. These experiences also caused them to highly value time alone. Therefore, they became observant, imaginative, curious, and inquisitive, and developed a love for learning—while also fearing depletion and the needs placed on them by others.

As Type 5s carry these tendencies into adulthood, they need to learn to rely on God to provide for them and meet their needs.

Knowing your personality Type's Childhood Message will help you break free from childhood perceptions and reinterpret pieces of your story from a better vantage point. As you explore this, be gracious to yourself and your past. Be sensitive, nonjudgmental, caring, and kind to yourself. And remember, only God can fully redeem your past. He can free you from chains that bind, heal wounds that linger, and restore you to freedom.

Going Deeper

*To what degree do you relate to the Type 5
Childhood Message?*

_____

_____

_____

_____

_____

_____

What stories come to mind when you hear it?

_____

_____

_____

_____

_____

_____

_____

What circumstances in the present have repeated this message from the past?

_____

_____

_____

_____

_____

_____

What advice would you give to your childhood self in light of this message?

_____

_____

_____

_____

_____

_____

_____

Enneagram Paths

The final directional signals we'll discuss are the Enneagram Paths, which the inner lines and arrows in the Enneagram diagram display. The lines and arrows going out from our Main Type point to our Connecting Types. As a Type 5, you connect to Types 7 and 8.

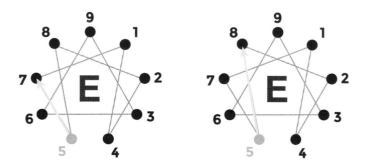

Remember, we can access both positive and negative characteristics of a Type we are connected to. The kind we access depends on whether we are aligned, misaligned, or out of alignment with God's truth.

Here is an overview of the four Enneagram Paths, which we'll discuss further in the following readings:

- *Stress Path*: When we're under stress, we tend to take on some of the misaligned or out-of-alignment characteristics of our Stress Path Type. For Type 5, these are the negative aspects of Type 7.
- *Blind Spot Path*: When we're around those we're most familiar with (mainly family), we display the misaligned characteristics of our Blind Spot Path Type. We typically do not see these characteristics in ourselves easily. For Type 5, these are the negative aspects of Type 8.
- *Growth Path*: When we believe and trust

that God loves us and that all He has is ours in Christ, we begin to move in a healthier direction, accessing the aligned characteristics of our Connecting Type. For Type 5, these are the positive aspects of Type 8.

- *Converging Path*: After making progress on the Growth path, we can reach the most aligned point of our Type, which is where three healthy Types come together. Here we access the healthiest qualities of our Main Type, our Growth Path's Type, and our Stress Path's Type.

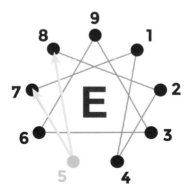

Going Deeper

In what direction is your heart currently heading?

_____

_____

_____

_____

_____

_____

What concerns are you wrestling with?

_____

_____

_____

_____

_____

_____

_____

What growth have you experienced recently?

When you look at the four paths, what path have you been traveling recently? Why?

Stress Path

Under stress, you tend to move in the direction of the arrow below, taking on some of the misaligned characteristics of Type 7. Learning to identify these behavior patterns can serve as a rumble strip warning that you're veering off course. Then you can

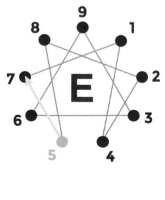

stop, pray for God's help, and move in a healthier direction for your personality.

As a Type 5 moving toward the average or unhealthy Type 7, you may:

- have a racing mind and become scattered, restless, and hyperactive.
- overbook your schedule with fascinating experiences and interests.
- take on too many new projects impulsively.
- become unfocused and distracted with too many new possibilities.
- be less patient with people.
- be cynical and jaded in your thinking.
- become talkative and impulsive.
- be erratically absorbed with learning everything at a feverish pace.

Going Deeper

Describe a stressful time when you took on some of these tendencies.

_____

_____

_____

_____

_____

_____

What was the situation, and why were you triggered to respond this way?

_____

_____

_____

_____

_____

_____

_____

When have you used numbing behaviors to cope with stress and feeling overwhelmed?

What tendencies do you notice about yourself in times of stress?

What things in your life cause the most stress for you?

TYPE 5 UNDER STRESS

When under stress, **Type 5** will start to exhibit some of the average to unhealthy characteristics of **Type 7**.

Becoming hyperactive and scattered

Taking on new projects impulsively

Becoming unfocused and distracted

Blind Spot Path

When you're around people you're most familiar with—family members or close friends—you
express yourself more freely. You show them parts
of yourself you don't show anyone else, for better
or worse. When you're uninhibited and not at your
best, you display the negative qualities of your personality. On this Blind Spot Path, you access the
misaligned attributes of your Connecting Type,
which is Type 8.

You may be unaware that you're behaving differently with your family members or close friends than
you are with other people. Be sure to take note of
this path when you're trying to understand yourself

and your reactions, because it may surprise you. Working on these negative aspects can improve the relationship dynamics with those you're closest to.

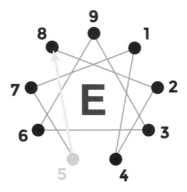

As a Type 5 moving toward the average or unhealthy Type 8, you may:

- assert your boundaries forcefully and confront anyone who displeases you.
- become feisty, argumentative, and provocative.
- become aggressive and vengeful if blindsided or betrayed.

- question others' competence while asserting your knowledge with strength and intellectual arrogance.
- argue or debate when facts are incorrect.
- arrogantly interject your thoughts and opinions.

Going Deeper

How do you respond when you feel overwhelmed in the presence of people you feel secure with versus those you're less comfortable with?

Which of the average or unhealthy tendencies do you resonate with the most?

Describe a situation where you reacted in the ways described above.

Growth Path

When you believe and trust that God loves you, and all He has is yours, you begin to relax and let go of your personality's constraints and lies. You draw nearer to Him and move in a direction that aligns you with His truth. You feel safe, secure, and loved.

Feeling more joy, peace, and liberation, you stretch yourself toward healthier attributes, even though it is hard. As you grow in faith and depend solely on Him, God blesses you with real and lasting transformation, shaping you into who He made you to be.

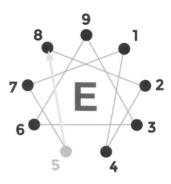

As a Type 5 moving toward the healthy side of Type 8, you can:

- become more self-confident, assertive, and decisive.
- be more active with your body, connecting with your emotions and gut instincts.
- trust your instincts, becoming bolder and quicker to take action.
- willingly take on responsibility, demonstrating courage and confidence.
- become less isolated and more grounded, capable, and competent.
- have quiet strength, endurance, and wisdom that others seek out.

Going Deeper

When you are growing, what changes about your
heart and your typical responses?

Which of these growth attributes would you love to
experience more in your life?

What helps to support your growth and flourishing?

How can you incorporate those things into your life more?

TYPE 5 DIRECTION OF **GROWTH**

When moving in the direction of growth, a **Type 5** will start to exhibit some of the healthier characteristics of a **Type 8**.

Becoming more self-confident and decisive

Getting active and in touch with their bodies

Trusting their instincts more; becoming more assertive

Converging Path

You are your best self on the Converging Path, where three Types come together. Here you access the healthiest qualities of your Main Type, your Growth Path's Type, and your Stress Path's Type. When you live in the fullness of who you really are in Christ, you are freed from the bonds of your personality.

This path of personal transformation can be difficult to reach and maintain. When you first learn about the Converging Path, you may feel it's too hard to travel. But God wants to provide this path for you. Trust Him, follow Him, and ask Him to be with you as you move forward.

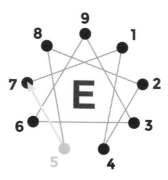

As a Type 5 moving toward the healthy side of Type 7, you may:

- enjoy life more, trusting God is benevolent and kind and will provide for your needs.
- become more spontaneous and physically active.
- enjoy a more exciting, abundant, and full life with others.
- allow your energy to flow and experience a lighter side of life.
- become more hopeful, optimistic, and joyful, seeing that life is full of purpose and meaning.
- become less cynical and more exuberant in trying new things.

Going Deeper

Can you recall a time when you experienced the freedom and joy of the Converging Path?

_____

_____

_____

_____

_____

What was it like when you accessed the healthiest aspects of your Main Type, Growth Path's Type, and Stress Path's Type?

_____

_____

_____

_____

_____

_____

What would help you move toward your Converging Path more often?

Spiritual Renewal

TYPE 5
THE ROMANTIC INDIVIDUALIST

GOING DEEPER

Grab a journal and write down the ways that God has been faithful, sustaining and providing for you throughout your life. Reflect on the truth that Christ is your living water that will never run dry.

Moving Toward Your Best Self

The journey of exploring your heart is not an easy one, but it's an exciting one.

God has a unique message for each Type. The message He tells you as a Type 5 is: "My vast resources can replenish you."

You will never be completely depleted, lacking the resources you need to survive. God knows what your specific needs are and addresses them personally.

You typically feel safe and secure when you have mastered a subject or have a deep understanding of a topic. The truth is you are already safe and secure in the knowledge that Christ has secured you as His beloved child. You cannot earn acceptance and love through knowledge; you can receive it from God. He freely offers you His unconditional love and help.

Each Type has a signature Virtue, which you exhibit when you are at your best, and Type 5's Virtue is *nonattachment*.

When you are at your best, you become nonattached to the constant belief that you need to hoard your time, energy, and space. You open yourself up and give your resources to bless others, knowing that God will replenish you when you are low on energy.

You also see the beauty of being a part of relationships, collaboration, and community life. You find deep satisfaction and joy in giving of yourself to others and bringing great change in the world as a result.

Using the Enneagram from a biblical perspective can empower you to see yourself with astonishing clarity so you can break free from self-condemnation, fear, and shame by experiencing unconditional love, forgiveness, and freedom. In

Him, you are whole. And with Him by your side, you can grow stronger and healthier every day.

Now that you know how to use this internal GPS and its navigational signals, start using it every day. Tune in to how your heart is doing. Avoid your common pitfalls by staying alert to your rumble strips. As you learn new awareness and actions, you will move forward on the path that is healthiest for your personality Type and experience the gift of tremendous personal growth.

Going Deeper

What do you notice about yourself when you're at your best?

What would the world be like without the involvement of healthy Type 5s?

Type 5 **VIRTUE**

Nonattachment is your virtue.

This allows you to have
profound compassion for all
living things because you see
their temporary nature.

What are some practical
ways you can offer your
virtue to others today?

Afterword

God's plan to restore the world involves all of us, which is why He made us so vastly different from each other in ways that reflect who He is.

That is why I'm so thrilled you picked up this book and have done the hard, but rewarding, work of looking into your heart. When you align with God's truth, you can support the kingdom, knit people together, and be the best *you* only you can be.

Growth is *not* easy. It requires us to surrender to God, depend on Him, and walk into His calling for us. But when we let go of our control and He takes over, He will satisfy our hearts, filling them with His goodness, and His blessings will flow into our lives and others' lives.

I can attest to God's transformative work having this ripple effect—reaching and positively impacting different parts of our lives and everyone we encounter. As I became more aligned with God's truth (and make no mistake, I'm still in progress!), the changes I was making helped transform my relationships with Jeff, my family, and other people around me. More and more friends, acquaintances, and even strangers were experiencing the transformation that comes from God through the tool of the Enneagram.

I can't wait to look back a year from now, five years from now, or even a decade from now, and hear about the ripple effects *your* transformation has created for hope, wholeness, and freedom. I'm excited about the path of discovery and growth ahead of you! What is God going to do in you with this new understanding of yourself and those around you? What are the things you'll hear Him whisper in your heart that will begin to set you free?

And how will your personal transformation bring positive change to the people in your life?

This is what I hope for you: First, that you will believe and trust in your identity in Christ. In Him, you are forgiven and set free. God delights in having you as His dear child and loves you unconditionally. This reality will radically change everything in you—it is the ultimate transformation from death to life.

Second, I hope that as you discover more about your Enneagram Type, you'll recognize how your personality apart from Christ is running *away* from your Core Fear, running *toward* your Core Desire, *stumbling* over your Core Weakness, and *desperate* to have your Core Longing met. As you become aware of these traits, you can make them the rumble strip alarms that point out what's going on in your heart. Then you can ask the Holy Spirit to help you navigate your inner world and refocus your efforts toward traveling the best path for your personality Type.

Third, I hope that God will reveal to you, both

in knowledge and experience, the transformative work of the Holy Spirit. With Him you can move toward growth, using all the tools of the Enneagram (the Levels of Alignment, the Wings, the Triads, the Enneagram Paths, etc.) to bring out the very best in you, the way God designed you to be. As a result, others will be blessed, God will be glorified, and you will experience the closeness of a Savior who will always meet your every longing and need.

May the love of Christ meet you where you are and pull you closer to God and others. And may you experience the joy of knowing His love for you in a deeper and more meaningful way.

Acknowledgments

My husband: I have to start by thanking my incredible husband, Jeff, who is my biggest cheerleader and supporter. He has helped me use the Enneagram from a biblical perspective and lovingly ensured that I expanded my gifts. Without his encouragement each step of the way, I never would have ventured into this world of writing. Thank you so much, Jeff.

My kids: Nathan and Libby McCord, you are a gift and blessing to me, and an inspiration for the work I do. Thank you for affirming me, being patient with me, and always believing in me. I pray this resource will bless you back as you journey through life.

My family: To my incredible parents, Dr. Bruce and Dana Pfuetze, who have always loved me well and encouraged me to move past difficulties by relying on the Lord. To my dear brother and sister-in-law, Dr. Mark and Mollie Pfuetze, thank you for being a source of support.

My team at Your Enneagram Coach: You enable me to be the best I can be as a leader, and I'm so honored to be a part of our amazing team. Thank you for letting me serve, for showing up every day, and for helping those who want to become more like Christ by using the Enneagram from a biblical perspective. Thank you, Danielle Smith, Traci Lucky, Robert Lewis, Lindsey Castleman, Justin Barbour, and Monica Snyder.

My marketing team, Well Refined Co.: Thank you, Christy Knutson, Jane Butler, JoAnna Brown, and Madison Church.

My agent: Thank you, Bryan Norman, for helping me navigate through all the ins and outs so that this could be the very best work for our readers. Your advice was most beneficial.

My publisher: To Adria Haley and the team at HarperCollins Christian, thank you for allowing me to share my passion for the Enneagram with the world in such a beautiful way through this book collection.

My writing team at StrategicBookCoach.com: Thank you, Danielle Smith, Karen Anderson, and Sharilyn Grayson for helping me create my manuscript.

My friend and advisor: Writing a book is harder than I expected and more rewarding than I could have ever imagined. None of this would have been possible without my most-cherished friend and beloved advisor, Karen Anderson. I am thankful for her heart, her passion, and her help every step of the way. You beautifully take my concepts and make them sing. Thank you!

About the Author

Beth McCord has been using the Enneagram in ministry since 2002 and is a Certified Enneagram Coach. She is the founder and Lead Content Creator of Your Enneagram Coach and cowrote *Becoming Us: Using the Enneagram to Create a Thriving Gospel-Centered Marriage* with her husband, Jeff. Beth has been featured as an Enneagram expert in magazines and podcasts and frequently speaks at live events. She and Jeff have two grown children, Nate and Libby, and live in Franklin, Tennessee, with their blue-eyed Australian Shepherd, Sky.

Continue Your Personal Growth Journey *Just for Type 5!*

Get your Type's in-depth online coaching course that is customized with guide sheets and other helpful insights so you can continue uncovering your personal roadmap to fast-track your growth, overcome obstacles, and live a more fulfilling life with God, others, and yourself.

VISIT YOURENNEAGRAMCOACH.COM/EXPLORING-YOU

The mission of YourEneagramCoach.com is for people to see themselves with astonishing clarity so they can break free from self-condemnation, fear, and shame by knowing and experiencing unconditional love, forgiveness, and freedom in Christ.